# Pay yourself

Steps to wealth.

By Sheka Mansaray

Revelation Publishing

Kingdom Revelation fit to print

# Dedication

  The rich rule over the poor, and the borrower is servant to the lender. Proverbs 22:7

  This book is dedicated to the lives of God's people to **Pay yourself** out of Poverty, hardship and work to Creating steps to wealth Creation.

Introduction

*"Bring the whole tithe into the storehouse, that there may be food in my house. Test me in this," says the LORD Almighty, "and see if I will not throw open the floodgates of heaven and pour out so much blessing that you will not have room enough for it."* 2 Malachi 3:10

We must agree, since our salvation is no longer based on works, but on faith in Jesus. But to be quite honest, as New Testament believers, 10% should just be a mile-marker on our giving journey. After all, God owns it all and no matter where we are as far as what we are giving, we should always be striving to give more.

My wife Nanah and I had a dream. We wanted to work toward true financial freedom or at list starting somewhere, In other words, we wanted to get completely out of financial waste even including our rent at that where we were and be in a position where we didn't need to earn a salary to meet our needs. We wanted to live a modest lifestyle on the income from our saving, investments and retirement. And be in a position to volunteer to serve in the ministry without needing a salary. But we had all kinds of questions. Where should we start? How could we stay motivated for so long? We knew reaching this goal would take a long time, but that by God's grace it was possible. We were encouraged when we learned that Proverbs 21:5 says, "Steady plodding brings prosperity." This revelation birth in my heart *"Pay Yourself"* We realized steady plodding was the way to reach true financial freedom. We needed to have a plan with a series of small achievable steps along the way. And we always needed to focus on reaching the next step.

Pay Yourself is easy to follow and is a step-by-step guide that will work for everyone, regardless of income. You may not reach the final destination, but with God's help you can make progress. And each destination brings greater financial health and stability. The answers two big questions—where am I financially, and what do I do next? The first step is to find out where you are.

Look at the map. There are seven destinations. Review each one and check off what you've already accomplished. Now, you know where you are. The next step is to determine what to do next, which is simply to focus on accomplishing the first destination you haven't yet finished. Complete each destination in order before proceeding to the next. This will help you focus, make steady progress and build a solid financial foundation.

This book "Pay Yourself" will save life and family. I can see you buying more and give to others in your life and their life will also prosper by Pay Yourself .

**Table of Contents**

1. Learn God's way & getting started...page 7
2. Benefits of Paying...page 11
3. How Your Money Can Grow...page 13
4. Major Purchases...page17
5. Rule of 72...page 20
6. Savings Options...page22
7. Pay Yourself First Action Plan...page 27
8. Action Plan my goals must count...page 28
9. Come out of your troubles...page 31
10. Give an Answer...page 32
11. Product and services...page 33
12. Gifts and talents...page 34
13. Ideas...page 35
14. Work...page 36

| | | |
|---|---|---|
| 15. | Package what you have...page 37 | |
| 16. | Money wisdom...page 38 | |
| 17. | Reverse Your Thinking...page 39 | |
| 18. | Increasing Your Earnings...page 43 | |
| 19. | Take charge of your money...page 45 | |
| 20. | Where is my money going? ...page 46 | |
| 21. | Basics goals extras ...page 48 | |
| 22. | Money Priorities...page 50 | |
| 23. | Act to make your money work for you...page 55 | |
| 24. | Set aside money...page 57 | |
| 25. | Managing your money...page 58 | |
| 26. | Budget Planner...page 57 | |
| 27. | Managing your money...page 62 | |
| 28. | Strategies to save money ...page 64 | |
| 29. | Save for your future...page 66 | |
| 30. | Pay yourself in Abundance Prayer...page 67 | |

## Learn God's way & getting started

Learn God's way of handling money

• Start using a spending plan (a budget)

• Save $1,000 for emergencies

• Begin giving Learn God's way of handling money God loves and cares deeply for us. And that's why the Bible has so much to say about money. It contains 2,350 verses dealing with money and possessions, and 15 percent of everything that Jesus Christ said had to do with it. God knows that from time-to-time money will be a struggle for all of us, and He wants to equip us to handle it well. The financial truths revealed in the Bible are practical and work for all generations and in any economy. Suggested resources: click on Navigating Your Finances God's Way small group study or Your Money Counts book to learn more. Start using a spending plan (a budget) We don't like to use the word budget, because it feels like a financial straightjacket that requires hours of monotonous bookkeeping. We prefer to call it a spending plan, because it simply enables you to spend your income on that which is most important to you. If you need to start one, click on compass spending plan to learn how. Save $1,000 for emergencies The reason for saving $1,000 for emergencies is because emergencies happen—the refrigerator goes on the fritz, the car brakes won't work. And if you have saved the money for emergencies, you don't have to pile up more debt to pay for them. Begin giving There are more verses dealing with giving than any other financial topic in the Bible.

Gifts obviously benefit the recipient, but in God's economy, gifts given with the proper attitude benefit the giver more than the receiver. "Remember the words of the Lord Jesus, that He Himself said, 'It is more blessed to give than to receive'" (Acts 20:35). However, generosity without an attitude of love provides no benefit to the giver. "If I give all my possessions to feed the poor…but do not have love, it profits me nothing" (1 Corinthians 13:3).

The Bible teaches that we should give to our church, the poor and needy and to those who teach God's word. Especially when we face financial difficulties, it requires faith in God to give generously. The Lord recognizes this and encourages us to "Bring the whole tithe [give 10 percent] . . . and test Me now in this," says the Lord of hosts, "if I will not open for you the windows of heaven, and pour out for you a blessing until there is no more need" (Malachi 3:10). This is the only instance in the Bible where the Lord invites us to test Him.

Purpose the Pay Yourself helps people identify ways they can save money and introduces savings options that they can use to save toward their goals.

Objectives After completing this book, you will be able to:

1. This book will Explain why it is important to save.
2. Determine goals toward what you want to save.
3. Identify savings options.
4. Determine which savings options will help you reach your savings goals.

1. What is interest?

	a. The percentage of money you have in your account.

	b. The amount of money you save when you open an account.

	c. The amount of money banks pay you for keeping money on deposit with them.

	d. The amount of money you pay in order to keep your money with a bank or other financial institution.

2. What is the Rule of 72?

a. A formula that lets you know how long it will take for your savings to double in value.

b. A rule banks and other financial institutions use to determine interest rates.

c. A formula to figure out how much money you can save.

d. A rule you can use in order to determine the annual percentage yield (APY).

3. Before investing, you should do which of the following?

a. Ask your employer about how you can invest.

b. Talk to your bank or a reputable financial adviser.

c. Open a new savings account.

d. Buy a house.

4: Pay Yourself First Instructor Guide

Money Smart for Young/ Adults Curriculum

4. This is an account in which you leave your money for a set term and cannot make withdrawals or deposits during the term.
a. Club Account.

b. Money Market Account.

c. Certificate of Deposit (CD). d. Statement Savings Account.


5. This is the product designed for investing money over a long period of time so that you will have money to live on when you are no longer working.

a. Bonds.

b. Stocks.

c. Mutual Funds.

d. 401(k) Funds.

## Benefits of Paying

The Meaning of "Pay Yourself First" What do you think it means to "pay yourself first"?

Paying yourself first means that when you get a paycheck, you put some of that money in a savings account before you pay your bills or buy things that you want.

• Increase Emergency Savings to 1 month's income

• Pay off Credit Cards Increase Emergency Savings to 1 month's income Keep adding to your emergency savings until you accumulate 1 month's income. We recommend adding half of your monthly surplus to your emergency savings and half to prepay your credit card debt. Once you've accumulated

1 month's income in your emergency account, stop adding to the savings and apply the entire surplus to pay off your credit cards. If you pay off your credit cards first, add the entire monthly surplus to your emergency savings. As you work on Destination

2, continue contributing to your retirement account up to the amount your employer matches. For example, if your employer matches up to 3 percent of your income, contribute

3 percent of your income to retirement because it is free money. But do it only if, and it is a big IF, you can still make steady progress on Your Money Map. If you can't, temporarily stop your retirement contributions until you reach Destination

4. Pay off Credit Cards Snowball your way out of your credit card debt, and here's how. In addition to making the minimum payments on all your credit cards, focus on paying off the smallest balance card first. The reason we don't recommend paying off the card with the highest interest first is simple—getting out of debt is hard and we all need to be encouraged by seeing the balance go down and finally to be completely paid. After the first credit card is paid off, apply its payment toward the next smallest one. After the second card is paid off, apply what you were paying on the first and second toward the third smallest

Benefits of Paying Yourself First  There are many reasons to pay yourself first. You can:

- Learn to manage money better.

- Save money toward identified goals.

- Improve your standard of living.

- Have money for emergencies.

What are some of the things people save money for? Write a response on paper.

- Unexpected events such as loss of job, car repair, or hospitalization.

- Down payment for a house, car, or other large purchase.

- College.

- Vacation.

- Retirement.

Now that we have looked at some reasons to save, let's apply some of those reasons to our own personal circumstances.

## How Your Money Can Grow

Making regular payments to yourself, even in small amounts, can add up over time. The amount your money grows depends on the interest earned and the amount of time you leave it in the account.

Interest is an amount of money banks or other financial institutions pay you for keeping your money on deposit with them. Interest is expressed as a percentage and is calculated based on the amount of money in your account.

Increase Emergency Savings to 3 month's income

• Pay off Consumer Debt (auto, student loans, etc.) Increase Emergency Savings to 3 months income

2, you have accumulated an emergency fund equal to 1 months income. Now, you are going to increase your emergency savings to 3 months income. Use exactly the same strategy recommended for Destination

Add half of your monthly surplus to your emergency savings and half to prepay your consumer debt. When you've reached the goal of three months income in your emergency fund, stop adding to it. Instead, apply the entire surplus to pay off your consumer debts. If you pay off your consumer debts first, add the entire surplus to your emergency savings until you reach that goal. Pay off Consumer Debt (auto, student loans, etc.) Consumer debt is all debt other than credit card debt, the home mortgage, and business loans. How do you decide which consumer debt to pay off first? The same way you decided which credit card to pay off first—snowball them! Continue making the minimum payments on all your consumer debts, but focus on accelerating the payment of your smallest higher-interest consumer debt first. Then, after you pay off the first consumer debt, apply its payment toward the next smallest one.

After the second one is paid off, apply what you were paying on the first and second toward the third smallest consumer debt, and so forth. The three most common consumer debts are auto debt, student loans, and home equity loans, including home equity lines of credit. To learn more click on auto debt, student loans, home equity loans. Auto Debt. Car debt is one of the biggest obstacles for many people on their journey to true financial freedom because they get out of it. Just when they are ready to pay off a car, they trade it in and purchase a newer one with credit. Unlike a home, which can appreciates in value, the moment you drive a car off the lot it depreciates in value. It's worth less than you paid for it. Take these steps to get out of auto debt:

(1) Decide to keep your car at least three years longer than your car loan, and pay it off.

(2) After your last payment, keep making the payment, but pay it to yourself. Put it into an account that you will use to buy your next car.

(3) When you're ready to replace your car, the cash you have saved plus your car's trade-in value should be sufficient to buy a low-mileage used car without credit. Student Loans. Student loans come from two sources: the government and private lenders. The government usually offers the lower interest rates because they want to encourage college attendance. They subsidize the loans to drive down the cost. The day always comes when student loans must be repaid. If you have more

than one school loan, consolidating them may be a good option. It may reduce your interest rate and lower your monthly payment

If you have $1,000 stashed away under your mattress for a year, it will still be $1,000 at the end of the year, providing that it has not been lost or stolen. Your mattress is not paying you interest for keeping your money under it. What if the mattress happened to catch on fire with your money under it?

### Compound Interest

Compound Interest  Now let's talk about the power of compounding. Compounding is how your money can grow when you keep it in a financial institution that pays interest. When the bank compounds the interest in your account, you earn money on the previously paid interest, in addition to the money in your account. But not all savings accounts are created equal. This is because interest can be compounded daily, monthly, or annually.

The first chart we are going to take a look at is the Annual vs. Daily Compounding chart.

- $1,000 compounded annually at 5 percent earns you $50 in interest at the end of the year. Interest has been calculated once, at the end of the year. This is more than if you had kept it under your mattress.

Refer students to the Compounding Interest Over Time chart in their Participant Guide. Describe how interest adds up based on how often it is compounded and how long it remains in the account.

- If you deposit $1,000 in an account that has daily compounding, at the end of the day you would have $1,000.14.

- The next day, the interest would be calculated based on the amount of your original deposit PLUS the previously earned interest – $1,000.14, rather than just $1,000.

- By the end of the year, you will have $1,051.27. The extra $1.27 does not seem like much, but the next chart shows how it can add up over time.

Saving $1 and $5 a Day You do not need $1,000 to see the power of compounding. The small amounts of savings add up.

Look at what happens when you save just $1 a day at 5 percent interest that compounds daily. At the end of one year, you made an extra $9 in compound interest. The real power of compounding shows at the end of 30 years. You made an extra $14,465.

# Major Purchases

Save for Major Purchases (home, auto, etc.)

• Save for True Financial Freedom (retirement)

• Save for Children's Education and Save for Business (if you want to start one) Save for Major Purchases (home, auto, etc.) To establish the order in which you will save for future needs, establish your goals and decide what are most important to you. This will help guide how you choose to allocate your savings. For example, you may already own your home, so won't need to save for a down payment. However, saving for your retirement, your children's education and starting a business may be your priorities.

You may decide to allocate your savings this way: 40 percent for retirement, 40 percent for the children's education, and 20 percent to start a business. Save for True Financial Freedom (retirement) Every year more and more companies break their promises to provide a pension to their employees. Social Security is projected to run out of money. The bottom line: don't rely solely on an employer or the government; you need to invest for your retirement. When investing for retirement I recommend a simple rule of thumb: First, take advantage of all employer matches, and second, invest in a Roth IRA or Roth 401k. If your employer offers to match your contribution, do it! It's free money. For example, if your employer will match up to three percent of your salary in a 401k contribution, make sure you put at least three percent in. It's that simple. If you do not have a match, or once you have contributed for the match, focus on funding a Roth IRA.

I am a huge fan of the Roth. Although your contributions to a Roth are not tax deductible, they grow tax free, and after age 59 ½, all withdrawals are tax free! I don't know what the tax rate will be in the future, but the government's deficit spending could force it much higher than it is today. This will be a huge advantage to using a Roth. Since there are limitations based on age and income level, check with your tax preparer to determine how much you can invest in a Roth. Save for Children's Education Paying for a college education is an opportunity for parents and children to grow closer to each other and to the Lord. As soon as children are old enough, pray together each week for God to provide funds for their education. Ask God for solutions that will eliminate or reduce the need to borrow. And then watch! He is eager to reveal Himself by answering our prayers.

It is a blessing when parents are able to save to help pay for their children's education. There are several educational savings options: state-sponsored 529 Plans and Prepaid Tuition Plans, Coverdell Educational Savings Accounts, and Roth IRAs. Each of these options has pros and cons. Log on to Save for Children's Education for an explanation of each along with links to Web sites containing helpful information on student grants and scholarships. Many parents and grandparents are not in a financial position to fund any part of their children's education. If you're one of them—don't feel guilty! You can only do what you can do, and this may be a blessing in disguise. When children are old enough, have them work to save for their college.

When students work to pay for college, they appreciate it more, are more serious about their studies, and develop a solid work ethic. Save for Business (if you want to start one) The reason for waiting until Destination 4 to begin saving for a business is that it is important to have your personal finances as stable as possible. When you no longer have credit card or consumer debts, your monthly expenses are lower. And having set aside three month's living expenses (at Destination 3), you have a margin in case you need income from the business during some of its lean months. This may surprise you: It is preferable to start your business before you buy your home. The Bible says, "Build your business before building your house" (Proverbs ) In other words, create your source of income; then acquire your home. One of the most common reasons for the failure of start-up businesses is lack of capital—not enough cash saved up. When you begin a business with lots of borrowed money, you invite added pressure to be profitable quickly. Many businesses require several years to become profitable. So, these are my recommendations:

(1) Be patient!

(2) Save as much as you need before launching your business.

(3) Use as little business debt as possible, and pay it off as quickly as possible. When you operate with little or no debt, you have more financial stability to weather unexpected challenges.

# Rule of 72

The Rule of 72 is a formula that lets you estimate how long it will take for your savings to double in value. This calculation assumes that the interest rate remains the same over time and interest is compounded once a year.

Here is how you calculate it:

• Divide 72 by the current interest rate to determine the number of years that it will take to double your initial savings amount.

72 ÷ interest rate = number of years

• For example, if you invest $50 in a savings account at a 4 percent interest rate, it will take 18 years for your initial savings of $50 to double.

72 ÷ 4 = 18 ( I know you don't like math you and I both) You can also find out how much compound interest you need to have when you know how many years you want your initial savings amount to double.

Here is an example of how this works:

• If you put $500 in an account that you want to double in 12 years, you will need an interest rate of 6 percent.

72 ÷ 12 = 6

Let's see if you can figure out the interest rate you need to double your money.

• If you want your savings account to double in value in 20 years, what interest rate would the account need to have?

Answer: 72 ÷ 20 = 3.6 percent

Now that you know about the benefits of saving and how money can grow, let's look at the different types of savings and investment options that you can choose from.

# Savings Options

### Savings Accounts

There are two basic ways to save money. You can open a savings account at a federally insured bank or credit union or you can invest your money. An important difference between the two is that savings accounts are federally insured and investments are not.

Let's take a look at savings accounts first.

Open a Savings Account  We have already seen that, with a savings account, you make money by earning interest. The bank pays you interest for the opportunity to use your money. A savings account also ensures that your money is safe and that you have easy access to it.

Activity 5: Four Savings Products  You are probably already familiar with some of these. What I would like to do is have you try to match the name of the account with its description. Do not worry if you do not know the answer. I will give you the right answers.

Buy an Investment  You've probably heard a lot about investing and how sometimes it can be good or bad. It is important to be well-informed before making an investment. You probably do not have the extra money to begin investing now, but you will soon and this information is very important for your financial success and stability.

An investment is a long-term savings option that you purchase for future income or financial benefit. Many banks now sell investment products, such as mutual funds.

- We saw earlier that while some investment products are sold at banks, they are not the same as deposit accounts because the money you invest is not federally insured.

- When you invest money, there is also a greater risk of losing it than if you put your money in a savings or other deposit account. In fact, there is a possibility that you might lose the entire amount you invest if the investment does not perform well.

- But because of the risk you take when you invest your money, your investment may earn and grow more than a regular savings account. In general, the higher the risk, the higher the expected rate of return on the investment.

You make money on investments by selling them for more than you paid for them, or by earning dividends and interest. The money you earn is considered income; therefore, you may have to pay taxes on it

Before You Invest  If you are interested in learning more about investment products, talk to:

- Your bank

- A reputable financial advisor, or

- An investment firm

When you become employed, ask your employer about any retirement accounts that are offered through your job. Retirement accounts, such as a 401(k), typically require you to be a full-time employee so you may not be eligible until after college or when you have a full-time job. You can also do your own research on investments. A public library or the Internet is a good place to start.

## Investment Products

Investment Products  Let's look at some more popular types of investment products that you can buy:

- Bonds

- Stocks

- Mutual funds

- Retirement investments

Most financial advisors recommend that, before you buy any of these investment products, you should have a savings cushion that will allow you to pay your expenses for two to six months. Any money you have saved beyond this amount can be used for investing. Because of this, you will want to wait until you are financially stable before investing. In case of an emergency,

sudden illness, or job loss, you always want to be able to support yourself.

While you might find this cushion hard to attain, even a small rainy day fund is important. So save your pennies now because it will all pay off when you begin your career and need to borrow from yourself for unexpected expenses.

## Investment Products

Let's look a little more closely at each of the investment products. We are not going to cover everything about these products today, just enough so that you know what they are and how to obtain additional information.

## How to Choose the Best Investment

Investments can benefit you financially, but you need to be well prepared and ready to take on the responsibility. Do not rush into any investment. Make sure you know all things to consider when choosing an investment.

Investment Issues to Consider Let's look at some strategies that will help you choose the best investment for you.

## How to Create a Savings Action Plan

### Decision Factors

Decision Factors You need to consider three decision factors when selecting the best savings and investment options:

• How much money do you want to accumulate over a certain period of time? You can figure this out by using the Rule of 72. This rule tells you how long it will take for your savings to double in value. It also tells you what interest rate you will need when you know in how many years you want your money to double.

• How long can you leave your money invested? If you have some money you will not need for several years, you might consider investment options such as stocks, bonds, or mutual funds. On the other hand, if you think you might need access to your money right away, it might be best for you to keep it in a savings account where you have immediate access to it.

- How do you feel about risking your money? As we have seen, if you are not comfortable with risk and cannot afford to lose the money, you might consider depositing your money in an insured financial institution. You will need to shop around for the account that best meets your needs.

# Pay Yourself First Action Plan

We are going to use the Pay Yourself First Action Plan to write down the action steps we intend to take to save toward our goals.

Savings Tips

General Tips

• Consider needs versus wants. Think about the items you purchase on a regular basis. These add up. Where can you save?

Do you eat out a lot? Can you cut back on daily expenses, such as coffee, candy, or soda?

1. If you receive cash as a gift, save at least part of it. (10%)

    When You Are on Your Own
2. Pay your bills on time. This saves the added expense of:
    a. Late fees.
3. Over draft from your card or account saving.
    a. Extra finance charges.
    b. Disconnection fees for utilities such as phone or electricity and fees to reestablish connection if your service is disconnected.
    c. The cost of eviction or repossession.
    d. Calls from bill collectors and collection letters.
4. Use direct deposit or automatic transfer to savings.
5. When you get paid, put a portion in savings through direct deposit or automatic transfer.

If you have a checking account, you may sign up to have money moved into your savings account every month.

➢ What you do not see, you do not miss!

**Plan my goals must count**

# Affordable Purchase

• Start Prepaying Home Mortgage

• Begin Investing Purchase Affordable Home There are two rules of thumb for purchasing an affordable home. First, put a down payment of at least 20 percent of the purchase price. This eliminates the need for you to carry expensive mortgage insurance (PMI) that protects only the lender.

Smaller payments also make it easier to afford larger prepayments, speeding up the day when you can burn your mortgage. And starting with at least 20 percent equity protects you from the becoming "upside down" on your home mortgage where the debt is greater than the value of your home. The second rule of thumb is your total housing expenses should not exceed 40 percent of your gross income. That 40 percent includes all housing expenses: mortgage payment, real estate taxes, utilities, insurance, and maintenance (estimate maintenance each year to be 1–2 percent of the value of the home).

If these combined expenses exceed 40 percent of your income, you will need to reduce spending in other categories. Start Prepaying Home Mortgage For most of us our home mortgage is our largest expense. Without a mortgage, we would enjoy greater financial stability. It would free up a big part of our income so we could give more generously to the work of Christ and invest more aggressively to reach our goal of true financial freedom. There are several ways to accelerate the payment of your home mortgage. If you need a new mortgage or the conditions are favorable for you to refinance, consider a shorter-term mortgage. If you can afford higher payments, go with a 10-year or 15-year instead of a 30-year mortgage. The interest rates are normally lower than the 30-year rate, and the outstanding balance shrinks much faster. You can also accelerate the repayment of your mortgage simply by paying an extra amount each month.

Contact your lender to find out how they want this done to ensure your prepayment is reducing the outstanding principal. Click on mortgage prepayment to determine how much you save and how quickly your mortgage will be paid off with various amount of prepayments. Begin Investing There are three biblical investing principles that are important to apply. First, the fundamental principle for becoming a successful investor is to spend less than you earn and then regularly invest the surplus. In other words, be a steady plodder. We've talked about this before. The Bible says, "Steady plodding brings prosperity" (Proverbs 21:5). Nothing replaces consistent, month-after-month investing. Regardless of the economy or investment climate—just do it. Second, seek the advice of a professional.

If you are not an experienced investor, we recommend that you use a financial planner or investment advisor when you begin investing. Use an advisor who understands what the Bible says about money because it will make a huge difference in the quality of their advice. If you do not know one, Kingdom Advisors is an excellent place to search. I suggest interviewing at least three candidates before choosing the one with whom you are most comfortable. Third, the Bible says, "Divide your portion to seven or even to eight, for you do not know what misfortune may occur on the earth" (Ecclesiastes 11:2).No investment is guaranteed, and money can be lost on any of them. The stock market, bonds, real estate, gold—you name it— can perform well or poorly. Each type of investment has its own advantages and disadvantages. Since the perfect investment doesn't exist, we need to diversify and not put all our eggs in one basket.

Action Plan What will I do now to save toward my goals?

What will I do by the end of **the week** to save toward my goals?

What will I do by the end of **the month** to save toward my goals?

What will I do by the end of **the year** to save toward my goals?

How are you going to make the money and who and what do you see fit to help you with meet your goals. And come to this understanding that money is connected to people.

Remember the more people you help the more your money grows, and Money is Hides in people and their Value.

## Come out of your troubles

Write three ways to come out of your troubles to help people in life.

1

2

3

## Give an Answer

What problems in life can you give an answer too?
Write three ways to help someone with a problem in their life.

Remember Money Hides in problem

1

2

3

## Product and services

What can you Product and services to others in need?

Write three ways to Services people in life.

1

2

3

## Gifts and talents

Write three gifts and talents you must help people in life.

1

2

3

**Ideas**

Money Hides in Ideas

Write three Ideas to help people in life.

1

2

3

**Work**

Money Hides in your work

Write three working Ideas to help yourself and people in life.

1

2

3

## Package what you have

Package what you have to get what you need.

Create your own products

**1st:** What does your financial picture look like?

**2nd:** What does Your Core Stream look like?

**3rd:** How Are You Generating A Stable Cashflow?

**4th:** What Are You Doing In Terms Of Savings & Investments?

**5th:** What Do You Want To Achieve Moving Forward

## Money wisdom

**First**
Build a simple financial plan for your future

**Second**
Setting Up Your Cashflow Management System And At Least 5 New Income Streams

**Third**
Identify & Eliminate Holes In Your Pocket And Unnecessary Sources Of Waste

**Fourth**
Create & Implement A Debt Elimination Plan

**Fifth**
Create and Supervise Your Investment/Savings Plan

**Sixth**
Heal Broken Relationships & Establish New Meaningful Relationships

## Reverse Your Thinking

We know: After taxes are taken out and the bills are paid, your paycheck can seem a little anemic — which can make the idea of having to save for retirement too seem like a real stretch. But to build wealth, a change in mindset is required. Namely, instead of spending the rest of your take-home pay, you'd actually take another cut of your paycheck and put it toward your biggest financial goals.
"Most people spend some money, pay their bills and save what's left," says Butler. "And that's backwards: You should be saving for your financial goals first, paying your bills and then consider spending the money you have leftover." Another trap is putting your good money habits off till "later," when life will get easier. The thing is, somehow the minute your income increases, the demands on your money seem to as well.

Now, keep in mind, we're not suggesting you sock all of your money away and live on rice cakes. As Blaylock puts it: "I'm not asking you to put $1,000 **(you can also put that amount away for you rainy-days if you have the amount)** away a month, I'm asking you to put away $50, or a small amount that you can afford. We really can't underestimate the power of starting small, because most of the time that momentum builds, and once we see progress, we tend to repeat behaviors."

### Look Where You Want to Go
Just as performance athletes imagine themselves making the shot over and over again — check out this study for how goal-setting improves motivation in

athletes — knowing what you want your money to do for you gives your goals a better chance of being reached

### Live Like a "Secret" Rich Person

For some, the image of a millionaire conjures visions of sprawling mansions and shiny Bentleys. But most millionaires don't live large like that — rather, they tend to live well below their **"means"** (noun: **means**; plural noun: **means**; noun: **means of something**; plural noun: **meanses of something**
an action or system by which a result is brought about; a method.
"these pledges are a means to avoid prosecution"

synonyms: method, way, manner, mode, measure, technique, expedient, agency, medium, instrument, channel, vehicle, avenue, course, process, procedure
"the best means to achieve your goal"

money; financial resources.
"a woman of modest but independent means"

synonyms: money, resources, capital, income, finance, funds, cash, wherewithal, assets; *informal* dough, bread, moola
"she doesn't have the means to support herself"
) and do more saving than spending.

## Know What's Coming in, and What's Going Out

Most of us have good intentions when it comes to saving money. But if you don't know what's coming into your bank account and what's going out, chances are you don't know how much you can devote to your goals. And most people generally don't track their income and spending, says Blaylock. "It really is shocking to me that clients I work with don't always review their pay stub," he says

## Getting Out of Debt

Everyone has debt at some point in their life. But if you have bad debt
— not student loans and mortgages, but credit card debt, where you're paying high monthly interest rates
— nixing it and getting out of the habit of being a debtor
— should be priority number one. "I want somebody to develop a plan to have them out of that debt in 36 months or less," says James. "It's hindering you from making progress on your other goals."

At the same time, emergencies happen — and a $600 car repair can hit anytime. That's why Blaylock advises putting half the money you could put into paying down debt into an emergency savings account. So, for example, instead of paying $600 toward credit card debt, consider putting $300 toward emergency savings and $300 toward credit card payments. While this means it will take longer to get out of credit card debt, you'll have money stored up for an emergency.

43

# Increasing Your Earnings

There are two ways to increase your net worth: Spend less or save more money. "And spending less is only part of it — you have to save, and when appropriate invest, the rest

• Avoid debt that does not help build long-term financial security. For example, avoid borrowing money for things that do not provide financial benefits or that do not last as long as the loan. Examples include: a vacation, clothing, and dinners out in restaurants. Examples of debt that helps build long-term financial security include:

    o Paying for college education

    o Buying or remodeling a house

    o Buying a car to get to work

• If you have paid off a loan, **keep making the monthly payments to yourself.** You can save or invest the money for your future goals.

• **Save your change** at the end of the day. Take that change and deposit it into the bank every week or month.

• When you get **a tax refund**, save it rather than spend it.

• If your work offers a retirement plan, such as a 401(k) or 403(b) plan that deducts money from your paycheck, join it! Most employers will match up to $.50 on each dollar you contribute.

    The matched amount is free money! Even if retirement is 45 years away, this is an excellent way to save. By starting young, you will be able to save more money than if you waited until you were older to start saving; thanks to the power of compound interest that allows money saved early to grow significantly over a longer period of time.

# Take charge of your money

Take charge of your money Want to know the secret to being good with money?

In just a few simple steps, you can take control of your money, instead of feeling like it controls you. Whether you have a little money or a lot, this booklet will help you:

1. X get off the treadmill of living pay-to-pay
2. X ease money stress and stay on top of your bills and commitments
3. X direct your money to where it matters most
4. X set goals so you can enjoy more of the good things in life

# Where is my money going?

Where is my money going day-to-day?

You may think spending up on big things is what gets you into trouble with money. But often it is the everyday little things that end up costing more over time. Where does your cash go each day?

It's easy to lose track of $5 here, $10 there. Do a spending diary The way to find out where your money is going is to do a spending diary. Make a note of everything you spend for one pay period or at least a week. This will only take a few minutes a day. You can do this just for yourself, or together with a friend or partner. Get to know your habits Tracking your spending is a reality check. It's not about judging yourself, it's about getting to know yourself better. By looking closely at your daily money habits, you will be able to make realistic choices about where you want your money to go.

Where is my money going month-to-month? Now you know where your cash is going day-to-day, the next step is to look at where your money is going month-to-month.

How much money is coming in? How much is going out? Think about where your money goes each month:

1. X weekly basics like food, groceries, transport
2. X regular bills like rent or mortgage, electricity, phone, insurance
3. X less frequent spending like clothing, holidays, car registration, medical expenses.

4. Do a budget The best way to take control of your household finances is to do a budget. This is a simple tool that helps you understand the money going in and out of your household. It shows you if you are spending more or less than you can afford. You can then take action to find the right balance between spending and saving.

Compare money in and money out

Managing your money Smart tip Use our free online budget planner Want your computer to do the hard work for you?.

Priorities where you want your money to go How do I make my money go where it matters most? The next step is to refine your budget and direct your money to where it matters most. This will help you find the right balance between spending and saving. How does a budget work in practice? It might sound simple, but using buckets is a good way to sort out your money priorities. Imagine you have a big bucket filled with water. This represents all your money coming in – the total income you entered into the budget planner. Then you have three smaller empty buckets to help you work out where you want your money to go. Of course you can't pour out more water than you have. So, with the amount available, you decide how much to put into each bucket.

Money in Money out NEEDS basic necessities – need these to live on WANTS lifestyle choices – want but could live without all income daily living expenses such as rent and food paying down debt, building up savings your spending choices.

# BASICS GOALS EXTRAS

Managing your money How to use the budget buckets First, put in enough money from your income bucket to take care of your needs. These are the basic necessities, the expenses you have to pay in order to live. Money in Money out.

1. Your take-home pay
2. Your partner's take-home pay
3. Centrelink benefits
4. Family benefit payments
5. Child support received BASICS
   Rent or mortgage
6. Food and groceries
7. Gas and electricity
8. Transport
9. Health care GOALS
10. Paying off debt
11. Building savings
12. Holiday
13. Car
14. Education
15. Superannuation EXTRAS
16. Eating out
17. Entertainment
18. Recreation
19. Personal spending or pocket money
20. Gifts and donations
21. Your take-home pay

22. Your partner's take-home pay
23. Centrelink benefits
24. Family benefit payments
25. Child support received
26. Rent or mortgage
27. Food and groceries
28. Gas and electricity
29. Transport
30. Health care
31. Paying off debt
32. Building savings
33. Holiday
34. Car
35. Education
36. Eating out
37. Entertainment
38. Recreation
39. Personal spending or pocket money
40. Gifts and donations

# Money Priorities

Managing your money Priorities your needs and wants Identify where you can reduce your expenses and save money. 20 minutes You will need:

X open your online budget planner OR the hand-written planner.

How to reduce your expenses First, highlight the most important things in your budget – your needs or basic necessities.

Then, identify the things you want but could do without, if you had to. What can you cut out or cut back? Switch or save Switch

X Are there memberships or subscriptions you could cancel or get for a lower cost? – gym, clubs – magazines, pay tv

X Is there a cheaper mobile phone plan?

X Can you shop around for a better deal on car or contents insurance?

X Are you paying for more health cover than you need?

X Could you switch to a super fund with lower fees? Save

X What can you get for free or cheaper elsewhere? – use the internet at the library – watch freeview instead of pay TV

X How could you spend less on groceries? – take a list and only buy what is on the list – look for home brand products and items on special – buy in bulk and only go shopping once a fortnight

X Can you reduce your spending on eating out? – make lunch instead of buying takeaway – have a dinner party and get everyone to bring a plate

X Can you save on your electricity bill? – switch appliances off instead of leaving in standby mode – use a fan instead of air conditioning – pay in instalments, so you have less to pay in one go Smart tip How to increase your income

X Are you getting all the Centrelink benefits you are entitled to?

X Could you earn more money from part-time work or hobbies?

X Do you have any unwanted goods you could swap or sell?

X If you have adult children living with you, are they contributing towards household costs? 19 Managing your money Smart tip Shop with cash instead of credit With a credit card, it is easy to spend more than you can afford. Keep in mind that a credit card is really a debt card. If you don't have the money to pay cash for something today, will you have the money next month when the bill is due, plus interest and charges? It is often easier to keep to a budget if you use cash, or a debit card when shopping. Try saving up or using lay-by instead of a credit or store card to make big purchases like a TV or washing machine. Pay your purchase off in instalments, and avoid extra fees or charges. List your savings and cuts Make a note of all the items you could cut out or cut back. Then check:

X Is this realistic?

X Do you need to cut back on all of these items, or just some?

X What are the most obvious ones to start with? Even if you need to reduce your expenses a lot, try not to cut out everything in your 'wants' bucket. By allowing yourself a treat now and then, you will find it much easier to stick to your budget.

Set goals for the future and make a plan to achieve them. 20 minutes Having worked out ways to reduce your expenses and save money, you are ready to start planning your future goals. What do you want from life? Why? Setting goals for yourself – whether large or small, short or long-term – is exciting and motivating. You may surprise yourself with how much you can achieve when you put your mind to it! What are some possible goals? Reduce your debt... Start to save... Pay off:

X your credit card

X a personal loan

X a car loan

X your mortgage Save for:

X a holiday or weekend away

X Christmas presents and celebrations

X a 'rainy day' fund, for big bills or emergencies

- X your wedding
- X a home deposit
- X your children's education
- X starting your own business
- X extra super contributions
- X your retirement

Managing your money Set your goals Think for a moment, then write down some possible goals. Now:

- X What is your top priority?
- X How much will it cost?
- X When would you like to achieve it? If you have borrowed money on a high interest rate, make paying off that debt your first priority, before taking on other goals.

Make your plan Be specific about what you want to achieve, how much you intend to save, and by when. If you would like to save for several goals at once, fill in these details for each goal. Make sure this is realistic and affordable.

Goal 1 What When How much

Goal 2 What When How much

Smart tip How to achieve your goals

1. Start small – begin with something small (for example, a weekend away or start an emergency savings fund).
2. Be specific – work out exactly what you want and why.
3. Be realistic – set yourself a reasonable amount of time.

4. Share it – talk about your goal with a friend, partner and/or children, to stay motivated.
5. Reward yourself – celebrate each step along the way to reaching your goal.
6. Managing your money Refine your budget Create a household budget that works for you. 20 minutes You will need:
7. your saved budget OR hand-written budget planner,
8. your list of identified cuts and savings,
9. your future goals plan. Update your budget planner Set your spending targets Go through each part of your budget in turn. Update the amounts in your budget to match your chosen cuts and savings. Add in your goal Add in the amount you are going to save for your goal (or goals). Balance your spending and saving Check that the way you have put your money into each category looks and feels right to you:
10. Have you been realistic in allowing enough money for your everyday needs?
11. Have you made enough cuts and savings to free up the money you want for your goals? If not, adjust your amounts until you are happy you have the balance working across all categories. Then save the new version of your budget and you are done.

## Act to make your money work for you

How do I make my budget happen? Now that you have your budget working, it is time to take the final step and put it into action. The trick is to make this as easy as possible for yourself, by making things happen automatically. That way you won't have to work at your budget – you will make your money work for you. Pay important bills by direct debit If you are regularly paid a salary or benefits, set up a direct debit from your bank account for the day after the money is deposited. This works well for things like:

1. rent or mortgage
2. personal loan or car repayments
3. paying off a backlog of credit or store card debt. If your income varies, or the bill amount varies, keep a close eye on your bank balance to ensure you have enough money in your account.
4. Start now – no matter how small the amount you can put aside.
5. Pay yourself first – get savings deducted from your pay or benefits automatically; most people don't miss what they don't see.
6. Keep your savings separate – put your savings into a separate account with no ATM access.
7. Add in your windfalls – try to save any pay rises, bonuses or tax refunds. Antonia and Rudi simplify their extras spending 'After doing our budget, we didn't want to try to track every

dollar in every category – especially personal spending. So we set up each member of the household (two adults, three teenagers) with their own cash card account, with a set allowance to spend however they like. Not only is this easier for us, our kids are now taking more responsibility for their spending.'

8. Smooth out your big bills Do you find that some months are more expensive than others – due to big bills, birthdays or unexpected events? Here's how to smooth out the ups and downs of your expenses. Mark your calendar
9. Go through your budget and highlight the big bills that come less often, like contents insurance, car registration or school fees.
10. Work out when (month/day) each bill is usually due. You may need to look back at the bills you collected.
11. Mark each bill on your calendar or a yearly planner – together with birthdays and periodic events – so you know when you are going to need more money.

## Set aside money

1. Add up how much your big bills cost in total for the year. If you wish, add an extra amount for gifts and celebrations.
2. Work out how much this is per pay or benefit period (for example, per fortnight).
3. Put this amount aside each time you are paid – by direct debit into a separate 'big bills' account or whatever works best for you.
4. Then you will have the money ready to cover the next big bill or special event. Ask about bill smoothing
5. Contact your utilities providers (gas, electricity, water) and ask about 'bill smoothing'.
6. See if you can arrange to make fortnightly or monthly payments to them, instead of having to pay the whole bill in one go. Arrange Centrepay
7. If you receive Centrelink benefits, ask about Centrepay.
8. This free service enables you to pay your utilities and other bills by having a regular amount deducted from your benefit payment.

# Managing your money

Stay on track After all your good work putting your budget in place, how do you ensure you stay on track?

CARE for your money

CHECK your budget at least once a year to see how you are tracking, and update amounts if you need to.

ADJUST your budget if your circumstances change (for example, if your pay goes up or down, you fall ill or lose your job, get married or start a family).

REWARD yourself with regular treats, so that living with a budget does not feel like a chore.

ENTHUSE yourself by putting a picture or chart of your goals on the fridge as a daily reminder. Go the distance If you keep your budget going, you can progressively achieve bigger goals, like:

1. going on holiday,
2. buying a car,
3. putting your kids through school, or
4. saving for retirement.

Taking charge of your money means less stress, more control – and a feeling of moving forward with confidence and ease. Now you know the secret to being good with money. A few simple steps really do make a difference.

# Budget Planner

Budget planner Understand the money going in and out of your household each month. 30 minutes Gather details of your income How much money is coming in?

Check pay slips, bank statements and investment statements. If your income is variable, make an estimate based on your past year's earnings. Gather details of your expenses How much money is going out?

Look at bills, bank statements, credit card statements, your spending diary, receipts and shopping dockets. Use your best guess if there is anything you can't find, or if bill amounts vary across the year. Put your income and expenses into the budget planner What is my current situation? Put your income and expenses into the budget planner. Adjust all amounts to the same frequency (this planner uses fortnightly figures)

MONEY IN: 1. Your fortnightly income Wages Your take-home pay

1. $ Your partner's take-home pay
2. $ Payments benefits
3. $ Family benefit payments
4. $ Child support received
5. $ Other* Bonuses/overtime
6. $ Refunds/rebates

7. $ Income from savings/investments
8. $ Other income

$ * Divide by 26 (amount ÷ 26) to convert yearly amounts to fortnightly. Add the above for your total fortnightly income

$ Budget planner Understand the money going in and out of your household each month.

30 minutes Gather details of your income How much money is coming in?

Check pay slips, bank statements and investment statements. If your income is variable, make an estimate based on your past year's earnings. Gather details of your expenses How much money is going out?

Look at bills, bank statements, credit card statements, your spending diary, receipts and shopping dockets. Use your best guess if there is anything you can't find, or if bill amounts vary across the year. Put your income and expenses into the budget planner What is my current situation?

Put your income and expenses into the budget planner. Adjust all amounts to the same frequency (this planner uses fortnightly figures).

MONEY OUT: 2. Your fortnightly spending* Shopping Supermarket

1. $ Fruit/vegetables
2. $ Other food/groceries
3. $ Baby products
4. $ Cosmetics/toiletries
5. $ Clothing/shoes

6. $ Pet products
7. $ Eating out Restaurants
8. $ Takeaway/snacks
9. $ Coffee/tea
10. $ Alcohol
11. $ Entertainment Movies/music
12. $ Bars/clubs $ Personal Personal allowance
13. $ Pocket money
14. $ Newspapers/magazines
15. $ Pharmacy/prescriptions
16. $ Gym/sports membership
17. $ Cigarettes/gambling
18. $ Transport Trains/trams/buses/ferries
19. $ Petrol
20. $ Road tolls/parking
21. $ Goals Savings
22. $ Extra super contributions
23. $ Other goals
24. $ Other Other fortnightly spending

\* Multiply by 2 (amount x 2) to convert any weekly amount to fortnightly. Add the above for your total fortnightly spending.

# Managing your money

Your monthly spending Home Rent/mortgage

1. $ Payments Car loan repayments
2. $ Other loan repayments
3. $ Credit card repayments
4. $ Child support payments
5. $ Communications Mobile phone
6. $ Home phone
7. $ Internet
8. $ Pay TV
9. $ Other Other monthly spending

Step 1 Add the above for your total monthly spending

Step 2 Multiply monthly total by 12 (monthly total x 12) = yearly amount

Step 3 Divide yearly amount by 26 (yearly amount ÷ 26) = fortnightly amount

Your quarterly spending Utilities/fees Electricity

1. $ Gas
2. $ Water
3. $ Council rates
4. $ Body corporate fees
5. $ Health Doctor/medical
6. $ Dentist
7. $ Chiropractor/physiotherapist
8. $ Other health

9. $ Vet/pet care
10. $ Education Childcare/pre-school fees
11. $ School fees

# STRATEGIES TO SAVE MONEY

**Housing**

1. Set your thermostat lower
2. Unsubscribe from your cable TV service
3. Turn off the lights when not in use
4. Get a roommate Live at home or with a relative

**Transportation**

1. Utilize public transportation
2. Carpool with a friend or family member
3. Ride your bike or walk Regularly
4. have your oil changed and use coupons for auto maintenance
5. Make sure your tires are properly inflated

**Entertainment**

1. Eat out less frequently
2. Eat early and take advantage of happy hours and early bird specials
3. Split or share meals with friends
4. Make your own lunch and bring it to work
5. Use restaurant coupons
6. Learn to cook dinner for yourself
7. Rent movies
8. Go to the movies in the afternoon rather than in the evening

9. Visit local libraries, museums, and parks
10. Participate in sports
11. Read a book or hike a trail

**Personal/Health**

1. Exercise
2. Don't smoke
3. Don't Drink alcohol in moderation
4. Give yourself your own manicure and/or pedicure
5. Use coupons or take advantage of specials for haircuts
6. Cancel unused club or gym memberships
7. Buy generic and OTC medications

**Debt Payments**

1. Stop using credit cards as a primary payment method
2. Pay off the full balance on each credit card at the end of the month

**Food**

1. Use a shopping list
2. Use coupons Compare prices
3. Buy in bulk Don't shop more than once a week
4. Don't buy what you can't or won't use
5. Miscellaneous Make a budget
6. Consider wants vs. needs
7. Don't spend money to relieve stress
8. Avoid impulse purchases such as coffee or candy
9. Give homemade gifts or give the gift of service rather than a retail item.

## Save for your future

four basic steps to secure their financial future:

1 Calculate how much money you may need for retirement or other goals.

2 Plan how to accumulate money and other assets to help meet your needs.

3 Act to implement your plan and save the money you (and your family) may need.

Your financial needs and the progress of your plan every year during the three month period between the time you receive your annual Social Security Statement and your birthday. If your needs have changed or your plan isn't working, readjust one or both of them. What are your financial goals?

How can you save enough money for the future?

Where should you begin?

These questions are enough to make anyone anxious. Well, take a deep breath and relax. Preparing for your future financial security can be challenging, but you can do it.

# Pay yourself in Abundance Prayer

Purpose: I wish to experience more abundance and more money in my life.

Step 1: Recognition God is everything that exists. All of the riches of the universe are present without limit in God.

Step 2: Unification I am one with the limitless supply of God. Everything that I could ever want or use is present in God, always.

Step 3: Realization Today I claim my abundant birthright. I know that I always have enough money to fully celebrate and enjoy life. That includes material wealth as well as an abundance of love, joy and rich, good health. Everything I need and desire is mine to experience now and forever.

Step 4: Thanksgiving I am so grateful for God's gracious nature! Step 5: Release I release this prayer into the Universal Good, knowing that it is done. And So It Is!.......

1. Oh Lord, baptize me with the generous spirit of a cheerful giver who gives out of love and not out of compulsion. 2. The Lord will make me a pillar of support for the expansion of God's Kingdom in Jesus name. 3. All my past generosity will be remembered by God. Every impossible situation in my life will be turned around by God on the account of my past generosity in Jesus name.

4. I believe in miracles, I serve a God of miracles therefore; every chapter closed by men against me will be re-opened by God in my favour in Jesus name.

5. Just as the famine in the days of Joseph elevated him, help me Lord to see the opportunity that the current global financial crises is creating for my prosperity in Jesus name

6. Oh Lord endow me with the required mental skill to interpret every opportunity that comes my way correctly and take maximum advantage of them in Jesus name.

7. I receive Grace to enjoy riches that will endure throughout my life time in Jesus name.

8. I receive total liberty from the embarrassing yoke of debt in Jesus name.

9. I receive total deliverance from the embarrassing stigma of knocking on doors and repeated phone calls begging for financial assistance in Jesus name.

10. I will enjoy the surplus of heaven to achieve my purpose and have leftovers in Jesus name.

11. Murmuring will not take the place of money in my life and money will not mess me up; all my bills will be supernaturally settled in Jesus name.

12. I refuse to be a burden on my neighbours, families and friends. I am a lender and not a borrower in Jesus name.

13. Whenever the needy need my help my purse will not be empty. I will be readily available to meet their needs in Jesus name.

14. Oh Lord, deliver me (my husband, my children etc) from the slavery of evil appetite/habit that are killing my health, money and destiny in Jesus name.

15. The Lord will satisfy my mouth with good things. I shall have appetite and money to eat choice foods and

accomplish great things in Jesus name.

16. I receive total deliverance from the curse of poverty and affliction that has ever plaqued my family line. I will live to transfer prosperity to my posterity in Jesus name.

17. I shall not only be great in wealth but also have a great name in Jesus name.

18. Let your Spirit empower me oh Lord, to attain, sustain and enjoy success in Jesus name.

19. My joy shall multiply at the end of this month... I shall therefore count blessings and not sorrows in Jesus name.

20. Oh Lord deliver me from profitless labour and confused activities in Jesus name.

21. I shall not waste my seed. I will be divinely guided to plant my seed on fertile soil in Jesus name.

22. Oh Lord, let the resources required to fulfill my dream in the custody of my enemies relocate into the custody of my friends and helpers in Jesus name.

23. Oh Lord, let money forever remain my loyal messenger in Jesus name.

24. Both the help from above and abroad will combine and compete to settle my bills and fulfill my dreams this year in Jesus name.

25. From now on all my investments and labour since the beginning of my career and ministry will begin to yield their full profit in Jesus name.

26. In every tight situation, let my tithe provoke heavenly solution in Jesus name.

27. This week my past generosity will spring forth a pleasant surprise in Jesus name.

28. Throughout this year, none of my resources shall be wasted on medical bills or any form of profitless venture in Jesus name.

29. Satan will not receive the backing of heaven to wipe out my financial resources with evil erosion in Jesus name.

30. Whosoever looks up to me for help this year will not be disappointed. I shall have enough to satisfy my needs and plenty to give to others in need in Jesus name.

31. I receive deliverance from the bondage of doubt and fear that past failures and misfortune has introduced into my life in Jesus name.

32. I receive the required courage to step into the greatness God has ordained for me in Jesus name.

33. I submit to the leadership of God's Spirit and I receive the backing of heaven to breakthrough and succeed in all my undertakings in Jesus name.

34. I receive the favourable countenance of God, therefore Heaven will agree with all my steps of faith and God's will shall prosper in my hands.

35. I refuse to submit my courage to frustration. God will send me encouragement today; I will be energized to continue the race in Jesus name.

36. The sun is rising today announcing my season of success and fulfilling my purpose in Jesus name.

37. Those that believe in me and have invested in my dream, encouraging and supporting me will not be disappointed in Jesus name.

38. The Lord will allow something better to come out of every bad situation that baffles me in Jesus name.

39. Let the prophetic power that operated in the valley of dry bones re-unite me with my lost (glory, helper, husband, wife, children, joy etc) in Jesus name.

40. Every carnal attitude of disobedience and demonic spirits that are promoting barrenness in my life are terminated today in Jesus name.

41. Those doubting my ability to succeed will soon become my subjects in Jesus name.

42. Those that refuse to lend unto me during my moment of struggling will soon begin to lean on me in Jesus name.

43. Those laughing at me today will soon laugh with me and regret their folly of looking down on me in Jesus name.

44. Those who gather to frustrate my vision will beg to be part of my celebration in Jesus name.

45. Every opposition I encounter today will soon form a chapter of my success story in Jesus name.

46. The Lord will release a measure of prosperity into my life that will swallow all my history of poverty in Jesus name.

47. The Lord will give me a new name and a new identity that will bury all the ugly stories associated with my background in Jesus name.

48. My new life in Christ has clothed me with a garment of righteousness; my past sinful life will no longer hurt or haunt me in Jesus name.

49. A similar grace that made Jabez more honorable than his brethren will distinguish me among my equals in Jesus name.

50. Today marks the beginning of my bouncing back. My spiritual life shall be restored and my lost glory shall be fully recovered.

51. I declare every department of my life under the control of Satan disconnected in Jesus name.

52. All the sinful habits that enslave me to Satan will henceforth irritate me in Jesus name.

53. In all the areas where men have failed me, let your mercy prevail for me in Jesus name.

54. In all the areas where money may disgrace me, let your mercy raised men of influence in my favour in Jesus name.

55. This week I will encounter God's mercy that will end all problems of money associated with my family in Jesus name.

56. Inadequate supply will not compel me to abandon God. Excess supply will not deceive me to disconnect from God in Jesus name.

57. I receive Christ Spirit of endurance to endure the season of adversity and wait for the era of prosperity in Jesus name.

58. The present adversity will not last forever; my business will not sink with the ongoing economic meltdown. The Spirit of God will usher in a new era of prosperity in Jesus name.

59. God's covenant of exception as it was in the land of Goshen will work in my favor against the ongoing economic recession in Jesus name.

60. Whatever positive purpose, I pursue, I will possess because the Spirit of God will instruct my steps in the right direction in Jesus name.

61. I rebuke the spirit of bareness from my business; my business will be fruitful and profitable in Jesus name.

62. The Holy Spirit will be the invincible Chief Executive Officer of my business in Jesus name.

63. I will not suffer scarcity of idea nor adequate capital to take my business to the next level in Jesus name.

64. The Spirit of God will expose and expel every Achan (traitor) among my employees that has the tendency of ruining my business in Jesus name.

65. The Spirit of God will deliver me from making recruitment error that is capable of crippling my business in Jesus name.

66. The Spirit of excellence, commitment, loyalty and uprightness will compel all my employees to work for the progress of my company in Jesus name.

67. Evil intentions and machination of my competitors will fail in Jesus name.

68. Every weapon sponsored through family relations or friends to wreck my business will not succeed in Jesus name.

69. I pronounce unstoppable prosperity over every project of my company in Jesus name.

70. Because this business is founded in partnership with God, it will take root downward, develop into branches and bear fruits upward in Jesus name.

71. I command a miraculous and total recovery of all debts owned by my company in Jesus name.

72. All my long-forgotten proposal will begin to receive the attention of the right and relevant authority in Jesus name.

73. The favour of God will envelope my company, office and shop in Jesus name.

74. Both my company identity and complimentary card will carry God's presence and attract favour of my prospective customers, clients and contracts in Jesus name.

75. I repeal every Local and International legislation that is not in favour of the prosperity of my business in Jesus name.

76. My business premises will not receive demonic visitation of armed robbers and dupes; law enforcement agents sponsored against me will not succeed at implicating me in Jesus name.

77. Partnership that will ruin my business will not receive my endorsement in Jesus name.

78. Agent of darkness on evil assignment against my business will receive God's judgment of blindness in Jesus name.

79. The economic policy of this nation will begin to favour the prosperity of my business in Jesus name.

80. The vision of the Government in power will not antagonize my business prosperity in Jesus name.